DISCARD

St. Therese School
Library

EASY COOKING

SIMPLE RECIPES FOR BEGINNING COOKS

Ann Beebe

ILLUSTRATED BY GAIL GARRATY

William Morrow and Company
New York 1972

Text copyright © 1972 by Ann Beebe
Illustrations copyright © 1972 by Gail Garraty
All rights reserved. No part of this book may be reproduced or utilized in any form or by any means, electronic or mechanical, including photocopying, recording or by any information storage and retrieval system, without permission in writing from the Publisher. Inquiries should be addressed to William Morrow and Company, Inc., 105 Madison Ave., New York, N.Y. 10016.
Printed in the United States of America.
3 4 5 76 75 74 73

Beebe, Ann.
    Easy cooking.

    SUMMARY: Instructions and lists of necessary foods and utensils for making a variety of simple dishes including cookies, candies, and sandwiches.
    1. Cookery—Juvenile literature. [1. Cookery] I. Garraty, Gail, illus. II. Title.
TX652.5.B35   641.5   72-155
ISBN 0-688-20038-9
ISBN 0-688-30039-1 (lib. ed.)

CONTENTS

INTRODUCTION   5

BASIC INSTRUCTIONS   6

COOKIES AND CANDY
Ginger Bars   8
Raisin Ginger Bars   8
Icing   9
Jiffy Chocolate Fudge   10
Pecan Treats   11
Marshmallow Crisps   12
Marshmallow Crisp Cups   13
Fondant   14
Fondant Balls   14
Coconut Fondant   15
Peanut Butter Fondant   15
Fruit Balls   15
Nut Balls   15
Peanut-Butterscotch Crisps   16

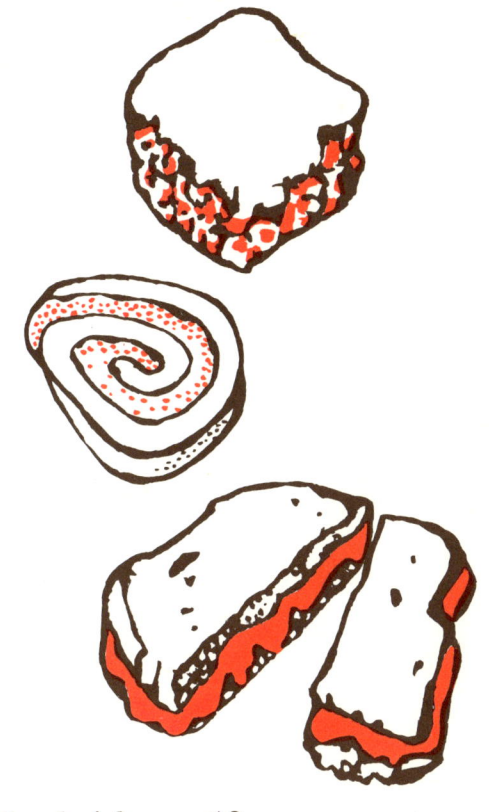

SANDWICHES
Cutting Sandwiches   17
Toasted Cheese and Peanut Butter Sandwiches   18
Hot Dogs   19
Nutty Hot Dogs   19
Toasted Cheese Muffins   20
Egg Salad Sandwiches   21
Tuna Salad Sandwiches   22
Peanut Butter and Celery Sandwiches   23

SOUPS
Clam Soup   24
Onion Soup   25
Tomato-Boullion Soup   26

CONTENTS

MAIN DISHES
Bacon Franks 27
Bacon and Cheese Franks 27
Oven-Cooked Steak 28
Saucy Ground Beef 29
Mushroom Ground Beef 29
Macaroni and Cheese 30
Tuna-Noodle Casserole 31
Noodle and Cottage Cheese Casserole 32
Acorn Squash with Sausage 33
Scrambled Eggs 34
Scrambled Egg Variations 35

BREADS AND PANCAKES
Biscuits 36
Cheese Biscuits 36
Cheesy French Loaf 37
Pancakes 38

DESSERTS
Berry Fluff 39
Choco-Mint Sundae 40
Peanut-Fudge Sundae 41
Strawberry Shortcake 42
Vanilla Peanut Pudding 43
Chocolate Peanut Pudding 43

BASIC FOODS
Broiled Bacon 44
Fried Bacon 45
Hard-boiled Eggs 46
Boiled Potato 47
Macaroni, Noodles, or Spaghetti 48

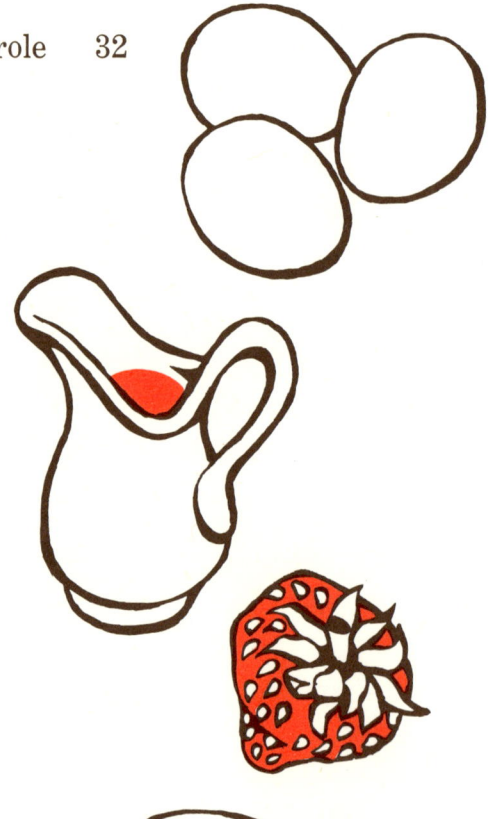

INTRODUCTION 5

TO THE BOYS AND GIRLS
WHO WILL USE THIS BOOK

This book has recipes to help you make foods to serve to your friends and family. Each recipe was chosen because the food is easy to make.

A beginning cook should plan to make *one dish* at a time. If you are to make the main dish for the family dinner, someone else should plan and cook the rest of the meal—vegetables, salad, and dessert—to go with your hot dish. If you are to prepare the dessert, someone else should make the meal.

This book does not tell you how to use the stove, broiler, toaster, oven, or other appliances in your kitchen, because they are all different. Be sure a grown-up shows you how to use this equipment. If the grown-up does not want you to use certain appliances, find a recipe that calls for the equipment you may use.

BASIC INSTRUCTIONS

BEFORE YOU BEGIN TO COOK:

1. Read the recipe to the end.
2. Be sure you have all the foods.
3. Be sure you have all the tools.
4. Be sure you know how to do each step of the recipe.
5. Get out all foods.
6. Get out all tools.
7. Wash your hands.

WHILE YOU ARE PREPARING FOOD:

1. Use a cutting board when chopping, slicing, or cutting.
2. Keep pot handles turned away from edge of stove.
3. Use pot holder.
4. Stay near the stove until you turn it off.

WHEN YOU ARE FINISHED:

1. Turn the burner and oven off after each use.
2. Wash all pots and tools you used; leave the kitchen as clean as you found it.

BASIC INSTRUCTIONS 7

HOW TO TEST AN EGG FOR FRESHNESS

Place egg in a bowl of deep cold water. A fresh egg will sink to the bottom of the bowl.

HOW TO SEPARATE EGGS (WHITE FROM YOLKS)

Cold eggs are easier to separate than those at room temperature.

1. Tap the center of the egg against the hard edge of a bowl to crack it.
2. Hold egg over bowl with large end down. Use thumbs to open eggshell. Lift off the top half, letting the egg white flow into the bowl. Keep the egg yolk in the bottom half of the shell.
3. Pour egg yolk carefully to the other half of the eggshell, letting the white flow out to the bowl.
4. Put egg yolk into separate container.

COOKIES AND CANDY

GINGER BARS

Oven

Foods	**Tools**
cooking oil or shortening	bowl
1 package gingerbread mix	measuring cup
1 cup applesauce	cooking spoon
	baking pan
	pot holder
	sharp knife

1. Set oven at 350.
2. Grease baking pan lightly with cooking oil or shortening.
3. Empty gingerbread mix into bowl.
4. Add applesauce. Stir until well blended.
5. Pour mixture into pan. Spread over pan bottom.
6. Place in oven and bake 20 minutes. Press *lightly* with finger. When done, gingerbread will spring back. If not done, bake for 5 minutes more. Test again. Bake until gingerbread springs back.
7. Remove from oven and allow to cool.
8. Icing may be spread on gingerbread (see page 9).
9. Cut into squares or bars.

RAISIN GINGER BARS

Follow steps above. After Step 4, add ½ cup raisins. Stir until well blended.

COOKIES AND CANDY   **9**

ICING

Foods	**Tools**
1 cup powdered sugar	measuring cup
1 tablespoon soft butter or margarine	bowl
1 tablespoon milk	measuring spoons
¼ teaspoon vanilla	cooking spoon
	spatula or butter knife

1. Measure powdered sugar into bowl.
2. Add butter or margarine.
3. Add milk.
4. Stir. Be sure butter or margarine is well mixed into the sugar.
5. Add vanilla. Stir.
6. If too thin, add more sugar and stir.
7. If too thick, add milk a few drops at a time. Stir.
8. Spread on ginger bars.

This icing may be used for other bar cookies or cakes.

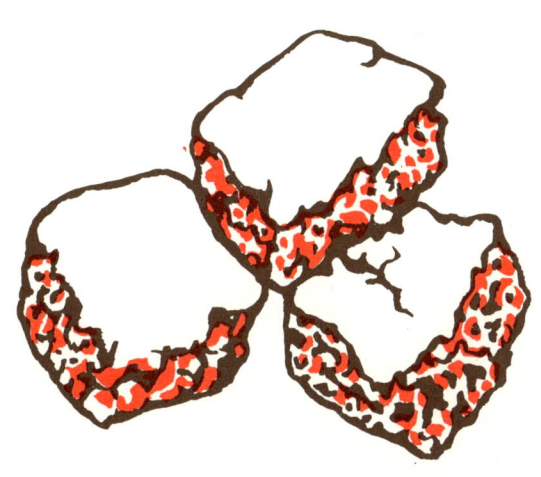

COOKIES AND CANDY

JIFFY CHOCOLATE FUDGE

Burner

Foods	**Tools**
butter	baking pan
2 6-ounce packages semisweet chocolate bits	double boiler
	pot holder
1/8 teaspoon salt	measuring spoons
1 15-ounce can sweetened condensed milk	can opener
	cooking spoon
1 teaspoon vanilla	measuring cup
1 cup chopped nuts (if wanted)	sharp knife

1. Lightly butter baking pan.
2. Pour ¾ inch water into bottom half of double boiler. Put on burner over medium heat.
3. Put chocolate in top half of double boiler. Place top half onto bottom half.
4. Melt chocolate.
5. Add salt. Stir.
6. Open can of milk. Add to chocolate and stir. Be sure mixture is well blended. (Chocolate bits form lumps, which must be allowed to melt.)
7. Remove from heat.
8. Add vanilla. Stir.
9. Add nuts, if wanted. Stir.
10. Pour into buttered pan.
11. Chill 2 to 3 hours in refrigerator.
12. When firm, cut into pieces.

COOKIES AND CANDY

PECAN TREATS

Oven

Foods
cooking oil or shortening
1 egg white (see page 7)
1 cup light brown sugar
1½ cups pecans, cut into pieces

Tools
sharp knife
baking sheet
eggbeater or electric mixer
bowl
measuring cup
tablespoon
pot holder
spatula
2 cake racks

1. Set oven at 250.
2. Lightly grease baking sheet with cooking oil or shortening.
3. Beat egg white in bowl until stiff but not dry.
4. Still beating, add brown sugar to bowl, one tablespoon at a time.
5. Add nutmeats. Stir with spoon.
6. Drop by tablespoonfuls onto baking sheet.
7. Place in oven and bake about 20 minutes.
8. Remove from oven. Use spatula to remove candies from pan.
9. Cool on cake racks.

Makes about 3 dozen

COOKIES AND CANDY

MARSHMALLOW CRISPS

Burner

Foods
1/3 cup butter or margarine
40 regular marshmallows
5 cups rice cereal

Tools
measuring cup
baking pan
pot holder
large pot
cooking spoon
sharp knife

1. Lightly butter the baking pan.
2. Place pot on burner over low heat and melt the rest of the butter in it.
3. Add marshmallows.
4. Stir until all marshmallows are melted.
5. Remove pan from heat.
6. Add cereal.
7. Stir until all of the cereal is coated with marshmallow.
8. Press into buttered pan.
9. Cool. Cut into squares.

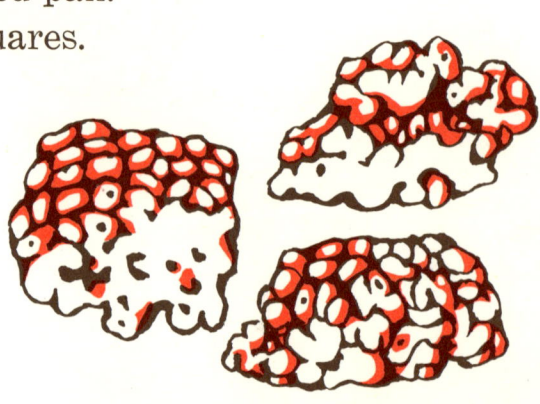

COOKIES AND CANDY   13

MARSHMALLOW CRISP CUPS

Foods
same as on page 12
ice cream

Tools
same as on page 12, except custard cups or muffin tins instead of baking pan

1. Lightly butter custard cups or muffin tins.
2. Follow steps 2-7 on page 12.
3. Use fingers to press onto bottom and sides of buttered custard cups or muffin tins. Do not fill cups.
4. Cool. Fill with ice cream.

Makes 12 cups

COOKIES AND CANDY

FONDANT

Foods
1 small potato, peeled and boiled (see page 47)
2½ pounds powdered sugar

Tools
bowl
fork
cooking spoon
covered bowl

1. Put potato into mixing bowl. Mash with fork.
2. Add ½ cup powdered sugar. Stir with fork. Potato and sugar form a liquid as you stir.
3. Stir in another ½ cup powdered sugar. Mash any lumps so the fondant will be smooth.
4. Add sugar ½ cup at a time. Stir with cooking spoon.
5. Fondant should be stiff enough to form into balls. Less sugar is needed if the potato is very small.
6. Divide fondant into 4 parts to make different flavored candy.
7. Put fondant into covered dish, and keep it in the refrigerator until you are ready to use it.

FONDANT BALLS

1. Add a few drops of vanilla, lemon extract, or maple flavoring to fondant (see above).
2. Work flavoring in.
3. Shape into balls. Roll in powdered sugar.

COOKIES AND CANDY 15

COCONUT FONDANT

1. Add ¼ cup shredded coconut to fondant (see page 14). Mix well.
2. Form into balls, or use to fill centers of pitted dates.

PEANUT BUTTER FONDANT

1. Sprinkle powdered sugar onto work table. Pat fondant (see page 14) into flat shape, about ⅛ of an inch thick.
2. Spread with peanut butter.
3. Roll into a long roll. Cut into slices.

FRUIT BALLS

1. Mix ¼ cup chopped fruit (dates, prunes, raisins, or fruitcake mixture) into fondant (see page 14).
2. Form into balls. Roll in powdered sugar.

NUT BALLS

1. Mix ¼ cup chopped nuts (walnuts, pecans, almonds, or peanuts) into fondant (see page 14).
2. Form into balls.
3. Roll in finely chopped nuts.

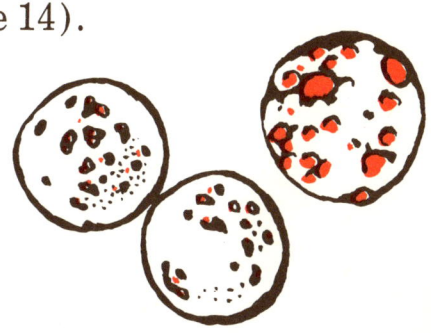

COOKIES AND CANDY

PEANUT-BUTTERSCOTCH CRISPS

Burner

Foods
3 cups Rice Krispies
½ cup peanut butter
1 6-ounce package butterscotch bits

Tools
measuring cup
large bowl
double boiler
pot holder
cooking spoon
tablespoon
wax paper

1. Put Rice Krispies in large bowl.
2. Pour ¾ inch water into bottom half of double boiler.
3. Put peanut butter in top half of double boiler.
4. Add butterscotch bits to peanut butter.
5. Place top half of double boiler onto bottom half.
6. Stir mixture often. When melted and blended, remove from heat.
7. Pour melted mixture into bowl with Rice Krispies.
8. Stir until all cereal is coated.
9. Drop by tablespoonfuls onto wax paper.
10. Allow to cool.

Makes 2 dozen

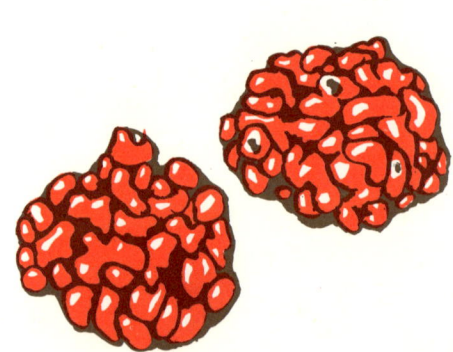

SANDWICHES 17

CUTTING SANDWICHES

Use two slices of bread for each sandwich. Lay the slices of bread out in twos on a cutting board.

1. Across, into 2

    Regular loaf

    French or rye bread

2. Crisscross, into 4

    Regular loaf

    French or rye bread

3. Diagonally, into 3

    Regular loaf

    French or rye bread

4. Vertically, into sandwich fingers

    Regular loaf

    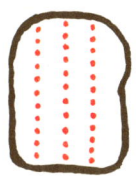

    French or rye bread

    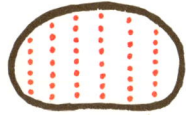

SANDWICHES

TOASTED CHEESE AND PEANUT BUTTER SANDWICHES

Toaster, Broiler

Foods	**Tools**
4 slices bread	spreader or butter knife
peanut butter	pot holder
2 slices cheddar cheese	sharp knife

1. Turn on broiler.
2. Toast bread in toaster.
3. Spread hot toast with peanut butter.
4. Place cheese on 2 slices of toast.
5. Put toast with cheese under broiler until cheese is melted. (Watch to see that cheese does not burn.)
6. Remove broiler pan. Top melted cheese with other 2 slices of toast.
7. Cut and serve while hot.

Makes 2 sandwiches

SANDWICHES 19

HOT DOGS

Burner, Toaster

Foods
2 frankfurters
2 long buns
prepared mustard
catsup
relish

Tools
pot with lid
sharp knife

1. Fill pot about half full of water. Place on burner over high heat.
2. When water boils, turn off heat. Drop frankfurters into water.
3. Put lid on pot. Let frankfurters stand 6 minutes.
4. Toast buns in toaster.
5. Pour off water.
6. Put frankfurters into buns.
7. Add mustard, catsup, and relish to taste.

Makes 2 sandwiches

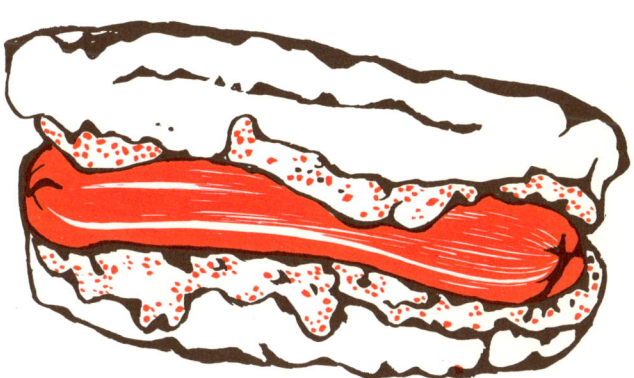

NUTTY HOT DOGS

Follow steps above. After Step 4, spread chunk-style peanut butter on hot buns.

SANDWICHES

TOASTED CHEESE MUFFINS

Broiler

Foods	**Tools**
2 English muffins	fork
butter for spreading	spreader or butter knife
4 slices cheese	pot holder

1. Turn on broiler.
2. Use fork to split English muffins.
3. Lightly butter muffins.
4. Place muffins on broiler pan, buttered side up. Put under broiler until toasted.
5. Remove broiler pan. Place 1 slice cheese on each toasted muffin half.
6. Return to broiler. Toast until cheese is melted. (Watch to see that cheese does not burn.)
7. Serve while hot.

Makes 4 open-faced sandwiches

SANDWICHES 21

EGG SALAD SANDWICHES

Foods
2 hard-boiled eggs
   (see page 46)
2 tablespoons mayonnaise
½ teaspoon prepared mustard
salt
pepper
4 slices bread
mayonnaise for spreading

Tools
small bowl
fork
measuring spoons
spreader or
   butter knife
sharp knife

1. Peel hard-boiled eggs.
2. Put eggs into bowl.
3. Use fork to mash eggs.
4. Add mayonnaise. Stir with fork.
5. Add mustard. Stir.
6. Sprinkle lightly with salt and pepper. Stir thoroughly.
7. Spread bread with mayonnaise.
8. Spread egg salad on 2 slices.
9. Top with other 2 slices.
10. Cut and serve.

Makes 2 sandwiches

22 SANDWICHES

TUNA SALAD SANDWICHES

Foods
1 7-ounce can tuna fish
1 tablespoon mayonnaise
4 slices bread
mayonnaise for spreading

Tools
can opener
small bowl
fork
measuring spoons
spreader or
   butter knife
sharp knife

1. Open can of tuna. Put into bowl.
2. Use fork to break tuna into flakes.
3. Add mayonnaise. Stir with fork.
4. Spread bread lightly with mayonnaise.
5. Spread tuna on 2 slices.
6. Top with other 2 slices.
7. Cut and serve.

Makes 2 sandwiches

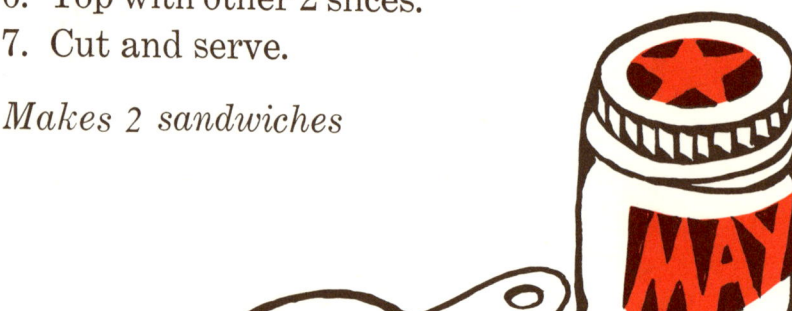

SANDWICHES   23

PEANUT BUTTER AND CELERY SANDWICHES

Foods
4 slices of bread
peanut butter
celery

Tools
spreader or
 butter knife
sharp knife

1. Spread peanut butter lightly on all 4 slices of bread.
2. Chop celery across the stalk. Chop it fine.
3. Put chopped celery on slice for each sandwich.
4. Top with other slices of bread.
5. Cut and serve.

Makes 2 sandwiches

24 SOUPS

CLAM SOUP

Burner

Foods
1 can condensed potato soup
1 soup can of milk
1 small can minced clams
1 tablespoon butter

Tools
can opener
pot
cooking spoon
pot holder
measuring spoons

1. Open can of soup. Pour into pot.
2. Fill empty soup can with milk and add to pot. Stir.
3. Put on burner over medium heat until hot but not boiling.
4. Open can of clams and add to pot. Stir.
5. Stir and simmer for 2 minutes.
6. Add butter.
7. Serve immediately.

Serves 2

SOUPS 25

ONION SOUP

Burner

Foods
- 1 cup chopped onion (or 2 tablespoons dried minced onion)
- 2 tablespoons butter
- 1 can bouillon or consommé

Tools
- sharp knife
- measuring cup
- skillet
- measuring spoons
- pot holder
- cooking spoon
- can opener

1. Chop onion. (Or use dried minced onion that has been allowed to stand for about 10 minutes in warm water. Pour off water.)
2. Place skillet on burner over medium heat. Melt butter.
3. Add onions.
4. Cook, stirring, until onions are lightly browned.
5. Open can of bouillon or consommé and pour over onions.
6. Fill empty soup can with water and pour into skillet.
7. Cook, stirring, until soup is hot. Do not boil.
8. Serve immediately.

Serves 2

26 SOUPS

TOMATO-BOUILLON SOUP

Burner

Foods
1 bouillon cube
   (or 1 envelope
   bouillon powder)
1 cup tomato juice

Tools
measuring cup
pot
pot holder
cooking spoon

1. Pour 1 cup water into pot. Put pot on burner over high heat.
2. When water boils, turn off heat. Add bouillon cube or powder.
3. Stir until bouillon is thoroughly dissolved.
4. Add tomato juice. Stir.
5. Return pot to medium heat until soup is hot. *Do not boil.*
6. Serve immediately.

Serves 2

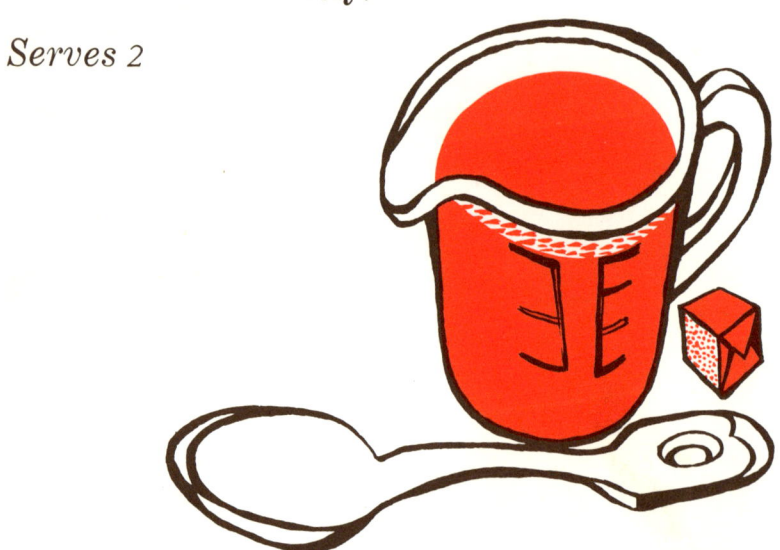

MAIN DISHES   **27**

BACON FRANKS

Broiler

Foods	**Tools**
2 frankfurters	sharp knife
sweet pickle relish	spoon
2 slices bacon	*wooden* toothpicks
	pot holder

1. Turn on broiler.
2. Cut a slit in each frankfurter the long way, but do not cut clear to the ends.
3. Spoon relish into slit in frankfurter.
4. Wrap a slice of bacon around each frankfurter.
5. Use toothpicks to hold bacon in place. They must be wood, because plastic melts.
6. Place frankfurters on broiling pan. Broil slowly, turning often, until bacon is crisp.

Serves 2

BACON AND CHEESE FRANKS

Follow steps above. At Step 3, instead of sweet pickle relish, place a strip of cheese in each slit frankfurter.

MAIN DISHES

OVEN-COOKED STEAK

Oven

Foods	**Tools**

Foods
2 pounds round steak or beef pot roast
1 package dry onion soup mix
potatoes and carrots (if wanted)

Tools
aluminum foil
baking pan
pot holder

1. Set oven at 300.
2. Place meat on large sheet of aluminum foil.
3. Place on baking pan.
4. Sprinkle soup mix on top of meat.
5. Wrap aluminum foil around the meat. Fold edges of foil over twice so that it is airtight.
6. Place in oven. Bake 3 hours.
7. If vegetables are to be added, remove meat from oven after 2 hours. Open foil. Add potatoes and carrots, which have been peeled and cut into pieces. Close foil. Return to oven for 1 hour.

Serves 4 to 6

MAIN DISHES

SAUCY GROUND BEEF

Burner

Foods
1 pound ground beef
1 can condensed pepper pot soup

Tools
skillet
pot holder
cooking spoon

1. Put ground beef into skillet. Place on burner over medium heat.
2. Use spoon to break meat into pieces.
3. Turn beef often until it is brown.
4. Tilt skillet gently. With a cooking spoon, take out fat. Put it into an empty tin can.
5. Add soup. Stir.
6. Add ¼ soup can of water. Stir.
7. Heat until the mixture is hot but not boiling.
8. Serve hot over noodles, spaghetti, or toast. (See page 48 for cooking noodles and spaghetti.)

Serves 4

MUSHROOM GROUND BEEF

Use 1 can condensed mushroom soup (either mushroom or cream of mushroom) instead of pepper pot soup. Follow steps above.

MAIN DISHES

MACARONI AND CHEESE

Oven

Foods
cooking oil or shortening
½ pound sharp cheddar cheese
4 cups cooked macaroni
  (see page 48)
milk

Tools
baking dish or
  casserole
sharp knife
pot holder

1. Set oven at 350.
2. Lightly grease baking dish or casserole with cooking oil or shortening.
3. Cut cheese into small pieces.
4. Put half the macaroni into baking dish.
5. Put half the cheese on top of macaroni.
6. Put the rest of the macaroni into baking dish.
7. Put the rest of the cheese on top of the macaroni.
8. Pour in milk, to just below the top of the macaroni.
9. Place in oven. Bake 40 minutes.

Serves 4 to 6

MAIN DISHES **31**

TUNA-NOODLE CASSEROLE

Oven

Foods
2 cups potato chips
4 cups cooked noodles
  (see page 48)
1 7-ounce can chunk-style tuna
1 can condensed mushroom soup
cooking oil or shortening

Tools
baking dish or
  casserole
measuring cup
can opener
small pot
cooking spoon

1. Set oven at 350.
2. Lightly grease casserole with cooking oil or shortening.
3. Crumble 1 cup of potato chips into bottom of the casserole. Add tuna.
4. Add noodles.
5. Open can of soup. Pour into pot. Pour in ¾ soup can of water. Stir.
6. Pour soup over noodles in casserole.
7. Crush the rest of the potato chips. Add to the casserole.
8. Bake in the oven for 20 minutes.

Serves 6

MAIN DISHES

NOODLE AND COTTAGE CHEESE CASSEROLE

Oven

Foods
cooking oil or shortening
1½ cups cooked noodles
   (see page 48)
4 strips cooked bacon
   (see pages 44-45)
1 cup cottage cheese

Tools
baking dish or
   casserole
measuring cup
cooking spoon
pot holder

1. Set oven at 325.
2. Lightly grease casserole with cooking oil or shortening.
3. Put noodles in casserole.
4. Crumble bacon and add to casserole.
5. Add cottage cheese. Stir.
6. Put in oven. Bake 30 minutes.

Serves 2

MAIN DISHES

ACORN SQUASH WITH SAUSAGE

Oven

Foods
2 acorn squash
1 pound sausage meat
   or sausage links,
   mild or spicy—*not hot*

Tools
sharp knife
spoon
baking pan
pot holder
fork

1. Set oven at 350.
2. Acorn squash are very hard. Ask a grown-up to cut the 2 squash in half.
3. Scrape seeds and stringy part out of the squash with spoon.
4. Fill each squash half with sausage.
5. Place squash on baking pan. Put into oven.
6. Cook 40 minutes. Remove pan and turn sausage so the browned side will be down.
7. Return to oven. Cook 20 minutes longer.
8. Poke squash with fork.
   If squash is soft, it is done.
   If not, cook until it is soft.
9. If there is too much fat, pour it off into an empty tin can.

Serves 4

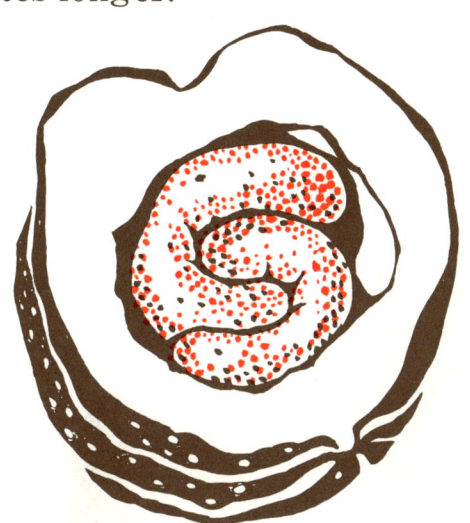

34 MAIN DISHES

SCRAMBLED EGGS

Burner

Foods	**Tools**
4 eggs	bowl
salt	cooking spoon
pepper	skillet
2 tablespoons milk	measuring spoons
1 tablespoon butter	pot holder

1. Break eggs into bowl.
2. Beat eggs slightly with spoon so yolks are broken.
3. Sprinkle salt and pepper lightly on eggs.
4. Add milk. Stir.
5. Place skillet on burner over low heat. Melt butter in it.
6. Add eggs.
7. With spoon, lift eggs from bottom of pan as they become firm. Turn.
8. Do not overcook. Eggs should be firm but not dry.
9. Serve immediately.

Serves 2 to 3

MAIN DISHES

SCRAMBLED EGG VARIATIONS

Add any of the following with the eggs at Step 6.

¼ cup cooked ham, cut into small pieces

¼ cup cooked bacon, cut into small pieces (see pages 44-45)

¼ cup canned mushrooms, cut into small pieces

½ cup grated cheese

¼ cup chopped cooked ham, mixed with ½ cup chopped onion and green pepper

½ cup cottage cheese

BREADS AND PANCAKES

BISCUITS

Oven

Foods
cooking oil or shortening
1 cup biscuit mix
¼ cup cold water

Tools
baking sheet
measuring cup
bowl
fork

1. Set oven at 450.
2. Lightly grease baking sheet with cooking oil or shortening.
3. Put biscuit mix into bowl.
4. Add cold water.
5. Stir with fork to make dough. Dough will form a ball.
6. Use fork to divide dough into 4 parts. Shape with fingers and fork into rounded biscuits.
7. Place on baking sheet. Bake 8 minutes.
8. Serve hot.

Makes 4 biscuits

CHEESE BISCUITS

Cut ¼ cup cheddar cheese into small bits. After Step 3, mix cheese into biscuit mix.

Makes 4 biscuits

BREADS AND PANCAKES

CHEESY FRENCH LOAF

Oven

Foods
- 2 tablespoons butter or margarine
- 1 loaf French bread (unsliced)
- 1 8-ounce jar sharp cheese spread

Tools
- sharp knife
- baking sheet
- measuring spoons
- spreader or butter knife
- pot holder

1. Set oven at 400.
2. Let butter or margarine become soft.
3. Cut loaf of French bread in half the long way, making 2 long pieces of bread.
4. Place bread on cutting board, crust side down.
5. Cut the soft bread every 2 inches. Do not cut through bottom crust. The slices will be held together at the bottom.
6. Place bread on baking sheet, crust side down.
7. Spread soft butter or margarine between slices and over the top of the bread.
8. Spread cheese on bread in the same way.
9. Bake in oven until cheese is melted and bread is crusty (about 15 minutes).
10. Serve hot. Tear slices apart to serve.

BREADS AND PANCAKES

PANCAKES

Burner

Foods
1 cup biscuit mix
1 egg
¾ cup milk
cooking oil or shortening
butter
syrup or jam

Tools
measuring cup
bowl
cooking spoon
skillet or
 electric griddle
pancake turner

1. Put biscuit mix into bowl.
2. Break egg into bowl.
3. Add milk.
4. Stir until mixture becomes a batter.
5. Lightly grease skillet or griddle with oil or shortening.
6. Heat griddle, or put skillet on burner over high heat until a few drops of water sprinkled on it jump around.
7. Spoon batter onto griddle into large or small pancakes.
8. When bubbles appear and burst, turn pancakes.
9. Cook other side of pancakes until lightly browned.
10. Serve immediately with butter and syrup or jam.

Serves 2

DESSERTS

BERRY FLUFF

Foods
1 cup berries
1 egg white (see page 6)
pinch of salt
1/3 cup sugar

Tools
measuring cup
2 bowls
eggbeater or electric mixer
cooking spoon

1. If frozen berries are used, thaw before measuring. If fresh berries are used, rinse berries.
2. Put berries in a bowl and crush them with a cooking spoon. Chill in refrigerator.
3. In another bowl, beat together egg white and salt until stiff.
4. Beat in sugar.
5. Add berries. Stir gently with cooking spoon.
6. Pour mixture into dessert dishes. (Fancy paper cups make nice dessert dishes.)
7. Chill in refrigerator for 1 hour.

Serves 4

CHOCO-MINT SUNDAE

Burner

Foods	**Tools**
12 chocolate-covered mint patties	double boiler
	pot holder
2 tablespoons milk	cooking spoon
ice cream	measuring spoons

1. Pour ¾ inch water into bottom half of double boiler. Place on burner over medium heat.
2. Put mint patties in top half of double boiler. Place top half over bottom half.
3. Melt patties. Chocolate covering melts first. Be sure to heat until the mint centers are melted.
4. Stir until smooth. Remove from heat.
5. Add milk. Stir.
6. Serve warm over ice cream.

If sauce hardens before serving time, put double boiler back over heat for a few minutes. Stir.

Serves 4

DESSERTS 41

PEANUT-FUDGE SUNDAE

Foods
½ cup chunk-style
   peanut butter
1 cup chocolate syrup
ice cream

Tools
measuring cup
bowl
cooking spoon

1. Measure peanut butter into bowl.
2. Add chocolate syrup.
3. Stir until completely mixed.
4. Pour over ice cream.

Serves 4

42 DESSERTS

STRAWBERRY SHORTCAKE

Foods
2 cups strawberries
½ cup sugar
4 biscuits, split and lightly buttered (see page 36)
whipped topping

Tools
measuring cup
bowl
cooking spoon

1. If frozen berries are used, thaw before measuring. If fresh berries are used, rinse berries and remove stems.
2. Put berries in a bowl and crush them with a cooking spoon.
3. Add sugar. Stir. Allow to stand 10 minutes.
4. Place bottom half of biscuit in dessert dish.
5. Cover with half the crushed berries.
6. Place top half of biscuit on top.
7. Pour the rest of the berries over all.
8. Add whipped topping.
9. Serve immediately.

Serves 4

Other fruit shortcakes may be made by using any fresh, frozen, or canned fruits.

DESSERTS 43

VANILLA PEANUT PUDDING

Foods
½ cup peanut butter
2 cups milk
1 4-ounce package *instant* vanilla pudding mix

Tools
measuring cup
bowl
eggbeater or electric mixer

1. Put peanut butter in bowl.
2. Add ¼ cup milk.
3. Beat until well mixed. (Use low speed on electric mixer.) If chunk-style peanut butter is used, mixture will be lumpy.
4. Add the rest of the milk slowly, about ¼ cup at a time. Beat until well mixed.
5. Add pudding mix.
6. Beat until pudding mix is well blended with peanut butter and milk.
7. Pour into dessert dishes.
8. Chill in refrigerator ½ hour.

Serves 4

CHOCOLATE PEANUT PUDDING

Use 1 package *instant* chocolate pudding mix instead of vanilla.

44 BASIC FOODS

BROILED BACON

Broiler

Foods
bacon, sliced

Tools
fork
pot holder
paper towels

1. Turn on broiler.
2. Place slices of bacon on broiler pan, side by side. Place pan about 4 inches below broiler.
3. Broil about 2 minutes. Using a fork, turn bacon.
4. Broil another 2 minutes.
5. If crisper bacon is wanted, cook a few minutes more.
6. Remove from broiler pan. Drain on paper towels.
7. Crisp bacon may be crumbled into small bits to add to scrambled eggs or casserole dishes.

BASIC FOODS   **45**

FRIED BACON

Burner

Foods
bacon, sliced

Tools
skillet
pot holder
fork
paper towels

1. Place slices of bacon in cold skillet. Put burner on low heat.
2. Cook slowly. With a fork, turn bacon often.
3. Cook until bacon is crisp.
4. Drain bacon on paper towels.
5. Crisp bacon may be crumbled into small bits to add to scrambled eggs or casserole dishes.

HARD-BOILED EGGS

Burner

Foods	**Tools**
eggs	pot with lid
	pot holder

1. Put about 2 inches of cold water into pot.
2. Put eggs into pot.
3. Cover with cold water.
4. Place on burner over medium heat until water boils rapidly.
5. Turn off heat and cover pot. Let stand for 15 minutes.
6. Be careful as you pour off hot water.
7. Cover eggs with cold water.
8. Pour off water again, and let eggs stand until they are cold (about 30 minutes). Eggs may be left in refrigerator in their shells until time to be used.

BASIC FOODS   **47**

BOILED POTATO

Burner

Foods   **Tools**
potato   knife
                                      pot
                                      fork

1. Wash potato under running water in the sink.
2. Cut potato into pieces. Try to keep pieces the same size. Cut a small potato into 2 pieces. Cut a large potato into 4 or more pieces.
3. Put pieces of potato into pot. Cover with cold water.
4. Place on burner over high heat.
5. Boil 15 or 20 minutes. (Small pieces of potato cook more quickly than large pieces.)
6. Poke potato with fork. When potato is soft, it is done. If not, cook until it is soft.
7. Remove pot from heat. Pour off the hot water.
8. Hold piece of potato with fork. Use tip of knife to peel off potato skin.

MACARONI, NOODLES, OR SPAGHETTI

Burner

Foods
- 3 quarts water
- 1 tablespoon salt
- 1 8-ounce package of macaroni, noodles, or spaghetti

Tools
- large pot
- measuring spoons
- cooking spoon
- pot holder
- sieve
- bowl with cover (if needed for storing)

1. Put 3 quarts of water in pot. Place on burner over high heat.
2. When water is boiling, add salt. Stir.
3. Drop macaroni, spaghetti, or noodles into the rapidly boiling water. Stir.
4. Cook at fast boil. Stir to prevent sticking.
5. Check for tenderness after about 8 minutes by poking it with a fork. When tender, remove from heat.
6. Pour into sieve over sink to let water drain off.
7. If not to be used immediately, put into covered bowl for storage in refrigerator.

1 cup uncooked macaroni or spaghetti (4 ounces) = 2 cups when cooked

1 cup uncooked noodles (2½ ounces) = 1½ cups when cooked

DISCARD

08

641.5
BEE
BEEBE, ANN
Easy cooking

DATE DUE			
MAR 20 1987			
MAY 12 1990			
MAY 19 2004			
MAR 29 2005			
NOV 01 2007			
DEC 06 2007			
JAN 29			

St. Therese School Library

641.5 BEE
Easy cooking :
201703